Ornament

PREVIOUS WINNERS OF THE VASSAR MILLER PRIZE
IN POETRY

Scott Cairns, Founding Editor
John Poch, Series Editor

Ornament

ANNA LENA PHILLIPS BELL

WINNER 2016 VASSAR MILLER PRIZE IN POETRY

University of North Texas Press, Denton, Texas

10   9   8   7   6   5   4   3   2   1

Permissions:
University of North Texas Press
1155 Union Circle #311336
Denton, TX 76203-5017

The paper used in this book meets the minimum requirements of the American National Standard for Permanence of Paper for Printed Library Materials, z39.48.1984. Binding materials have been chosen for durability.

Library of Congress Cataloging-in-Publication Data

Names: Bell, Anna Lena Phillips, 1978– author.
Title: Ornament / Anna Lena Phillips Bell.
Other titles: Vassar Miller prize in poetry series ; no. 24.
Description: Denton, Texas : University of North Texas Press, [2017] |
   Series: Number 24 in the Vassar Miller prize in poetry series | Winner
   Vassar Miller Prize in Poetry, 2016.
Identifiers: LCCN 2016041892| ISBN 9781574416657 (pbk. : alk. paper) | ISBN
   9781574416787 (ebook)
Subjects: | LCGFT: Poetry.
Classification: LCC PS3602.E448 A6 2017 | DDC 811/.6—dc23
LC record available at https://lccn.loc.gov/2016041892

Ornament is Number 24 in the Vassar Miller Poetry Prize Series

The electronic edition of this book was made possible by the support of the Vick Family Foundation.

Text design and typeset by Rose Design

for my parents
and for the Piedmont

Contents

Acknowledgments

I'm thankful to the editors of the publications in which these poems have appeared, sometimes in slightly different form:

32 Poems: "Midafternoon," "Qualifications for One to Be Climbed by a Vine"

The Anthology of Appalachian Writers, Vol. III: "When the Fire Comes Down from Heaven"

The Arkansas International: "Dishwashing," "Nesting," "Pears"

Birmingham Poetry Review: "Overture"

Canary: "Trillium" (reprint)

Chautauqua: "Hush," "June Swim," "Roustabout"

District Lit: "Girl at the State Line," "Girl at the State Line," "Sprout Wings and Fly"

The Fourth River: "Unhomemaking"

The Hopkins Review: "Honeysuckle"

International Poetry Review: "To Do in the New Year"

The MacGuffin: "Bonaparte Crossing the Rhine"

Michigan Quarterly Review: "*Limax maximus*"

The Nazim Hikmet Poetry Festival anthology, vol. 4: "And Not Look Back," "I'm Going Back to North Carolina," "Unfinished Story"

Poemeleon: "Green Man"

Poetry International: "Green Man" (reprint); "Strapless," "Sunday"

Raintown Review: "Trifoliate Orange"

Redux: "To Do in the New Year" (reprint)

Salt: "Mapping" (reprint)

The Southern Poetry Anthology, Vol. VII: North Carolina: "And Not Look Back," "Early Blackberries" (reprints)

Southern Poetry Review: "The Royal Typewriter Company Delivers by Parachute, 1927"

The Southern Review: "Ornament"

Think: "Piedmont"

My sincere thanks to the North Carolina Arts Council, the Durham County Arts Council, the Southern Women Writers Conference, the West Chester Poetry Conference, and the Dorothy Sargent Rosenberg Memorial Fund for fellowships, awards, and scholarships that supported the making of these poems. My gratitude as well to the Weymouth Center for Arts and Humanities, the Rensing Center, and the Virginia Center for the Creative Arts.

To the editors who have supported this book, thank you: John Poch, for incisive, thoughtful editing that improved the manuscript and helped me see it anew; Geoff Brock, for saying yes, and for generous thoughts on several of the poems; Karen DeVinney at UNT Press, for careful editing and for bringing a kind, wise attention to the entire publication process; and to the entire UNT Press team. Thanks to George David Clark, Jessica Faust, Ilya Kaminsky, James Smith, and the editors of all the magazines and anthologies listed above, whose thought, care, and effort deserve mighty praise.

Deep gratitude to the poets who've taught me, especially Carolyn Beard Whitlow, Sarah Hannah, Annie Finch, and Molly Peacock. For immensely helpful thoughts on this manuscript or on poems within it, thanks to Nellie Bellows, Lesley Wheeler, Tom Cable, Molly Tenenbaum, Catherine Tufariello, Timothy Steele, David Barber, Daniel Tobin, Bill Knott, Jim Hood, and Kim Addonizio.

Acknowledgments

For friendship and encouragement over the years this book was in the making, particular thanks to Bob and Deborah Cumming, Gabriel Cumming, Huma McAuley, Eric and Heather Nadel, David Schoonmaker, Jessi Slavich, Dane Summers, and Erica Yamaguchi; for the same, plus invaluable help with the science, thanks to Elsa Youngsteadt, Rick Fox, and Maureen McCauley; and many thanks to my stellar and generous colleagues at UNC Wilmington. Big thanks to Steve Terrill, Beverly Smith, Molly Stouten, and Brad Leftwich; and with gratitude to the many musicians, here and gone, whose playing is part of my life.

Thanks to my family in SC, NC, and OR, for their love and support—and especially to my parents, Sharon and Robert Phillips, for first showing me what it can mean to live with the land. Uncountable thanks to Tisko Tansi, roustabout.

Always, my love and thanks to Allen Phillips Bell, my love, companion, friend, and first reader. Always, to Meher Baba.

Ornament

Come on, pretty baby,
Just say you'll be mine.
We'll do that Tennessee shuffle on the old state line.
                                        —*Virgil Anderson*

Midafternoon

Walking the empty house
after a friend has gone—
nosy in my own space,
watching the rooms return,

slowly resettling
into their daily selves,
as if, seen by other eyes,
the floor, the chairs and shelves,

the paths I walk between them
and objects on them show
the brighter, clearer form—
here shabbiness, here halo—

they wear for those who visit,
for eyes that don't expend
as much sight on their sight
and see the sum of them

not dimmed by repetition,
not clotted with contempt.
In these now-hallowed rooms,
however full, unkempt,

I want to rest, to float—
a dust mote in a beam
of light squared by a window—
to sigh and lilt between

the object and the eye,
before the day can catch me
back up into myself,
and through that prism, watch me:

as I am in the house,
as I am, of the rooms—
as, in another's kinder eyes,
what had been dull dust gleams.

Qualifications for One to Be Climbed by a Vine

If not utter stillness, at least dedication
to sloth; if not sandpaper surface, the texture
of knotty fenceposts, or the trees they were made from.
Resistance to gravity—if not pure vertical,
angling up, and so closer to sunlight.
When, wavering, greenest of greenest, a curling
shoot chooses its tangent from rootstock to leafout,
I wonder if I should stand straighter, stiller,
or stretch out a finger to capture the waggle
of winnowing vinetip.
                Which one would it wend to?
I channel the light-pole, the stake and the slender
gray post of old cedar, the wire that connects it
to others a vine could extend its new tendrils
around over hours, or days—could I stand it?
Stand still and stay put for enough of a lifetime
for waver to wander toward me and find me,
describe me, in spirals, as road leading sunward?

Trillium

They grow down in the bottom, where the deer
lie down in grass and leave their bodies' echoes
on the ground. Each year, the trillium send

three leaves and then three petals into the air.
We headed down the bank, past thorns and stones
that hold the bridge upright. My brother swung

along the creek, and brushed past three-leaved stems,
red-veined—"You'll catch poison ivy," I called.
"It's elder, Annie, it's a tree," he said,

and swooped past me—loped along in twilight,
shadows dismantled by his boots. I followed,
elder. Where the water bends to the hollow,

we ducked into a deer track, left the creek
night-talking. Silky grass swallowed our footsteps
and branches snatched at our eyes. The narrow path

came wider by the clearing. "This is where
the deer sleep, right?" he whispered. "In the day,
yes," I said. But when deer bark in the night,

it looks like this: our eyes, kept closed against branches,
opened slowly to a shimmering white,
flower sleeves that lit themselves and flared

over dark leaves. Like stars, whose light is both
a wailed call and calm response, they leapt
out from shadow as we leaned down to breathe

the barest scent of pepper from their centers
and walked among green leaf and flame-white petal,
careful that our feet did not catch fire.

Ornament

Make me down a pallet on your floor.
　　　—Mississippi John Hurt

Is mine a gaudy God,
one of bobbins, pins?
Are you of salt and sod
or mine, a gaudy God
who—fingers thimble-shod,
baubled, bezelled—begins—
be mine, a gaudy God,
one of bobbins, pins.

Are you of salt and sod,
a fish, an element?
Do leaves fall where you've trod—
are you of salt and sod
and span of milkweed pod,
seed-sailing filament?
Are you of salt and sod,
a fish, an element?

Do leaves fall where you've trod?
Do you call the forest yours,
make down a meadow bed?
Do leaves fall where you've trod,
your hands brush goldenrod,
your lips, with deer, meet pears?
Do leaves fall where you've trod?
Is all the forest yours?

Make down a meadow bed.
Make me your only own.
Be mine, a gaudy God—
make down a meadow bed
with moss beneath your head,
soft sheets to slumber on.
Make down a meadow bed;
make me your own.

Piedmont

If a piece of country is possibly exotic and possibly not—if it is
so enigmatic that no one can say whether it has come from near
or far—it is known as suspect terrane.

　　　　　　　　　　　　　　　　　　—John McPhee

Made as seas receded, transgressed, receded,
continents rifting, verging, proto-Atlantic
surging, laying silt down over mystery:
suspect terrane,

island arc, perhaps Baltic: no one yet has
named its origin. Slate Belt jostled next to
North America, fine fragments eroding,
metamorphosing,

now eroding again, till plates thrust-faulted,
shoving clastics and granite inland, compressing,
stiff sheets finally levered skyward, forming
all Appalachia—

layered, folded, Valley and Ridge still sloping
eastward, shifting, as plates pulled back, let in the
present Atlantic, lapping at just-made coastline,
as from the mountains,

Deep and Dan, the two newborn river basins
sluiced fine particles seaward, scattered them over
belts that now cinch the east coast's widest girth,
nestled together

next to ancient mountains, littoral plain:

undulant, layered over bedrock up to
rich surface: no sand remaining, or fossil,
only brown earth and

sticky red saprolite, ancient rock turned soft,
sweet with worm castings, leaves, new humus in which
poplar and oak trees thrive, their understory
filled with may apple,

trout lily, lichen, tree ears, ginger, trillium.
Stranded north of the foothills' farthest reaches,
I measure out those syllables once more:
piedmont my cure, my

charm against cold—but now my longing is dulled,
alluvial fan obscured by the sediment of
countless repetitions, wavering accent
strengthening only

when I'm back where inflection won't help pick me
out among strangers, where we must remember
each friend or otherwise by better shorthand:
this one for laughter

tinkling at the edges of meanness; this one for
kind words; this one for collards; one for poundcake,
pecans sunk to the bottom; one for her polydactyl
kitten—each symbol

works harder than it should have to, even the
cat with her many extra toes. The name can't
name the whole, so one of these facts, symbol or
soul, becomes facile—

still I edge up sideways, hopeful, gathering
paraphrases, endearments—*sister, sweetheart,*
grandpa, trouble, lives-up-the-road, my honey,
tall drink a water,

sugar—maybe you'll find a new one in there,
one to speak alongside the familiar *upstate*
and, if you get lucky, a name absent
sinister nothings

sung in *Will my soul pass through the Southland?*,
false nostalgia staining both past and present.
Always wanting the cradle of lowlands, creekbank,
needing to leave the

unquiet graves people keep making of them—
midlands or *foothills*, I have known no ballad for
Long Cane Creek, or the Saluda, no name that
holds every hollow,

so I keep this word for the dappled sash that
runs between Appalachia and once-African
continental shelf at sea level; westward,
signature buried

fossil deep. It can't be enough; it will be
plenty. Let my beloved be enigmatic—
memory's sharpest when the thing remembered
grows distant from us—

so, swiftly as possible, call each a name
fit for speaking: Blue Ridge, Oconee, Slate Belt,
River Bend, Chatham, Abbeville, North and, yes,
South Carolina.

Pears

Where cloven tracks dent the deep black sandy soil,
turned faintly pink in early evening light,
I duck beneath the low brows of the trees
and turn the windfalls over in my hands.
Pale, articulate wounds break the rough brown coats.
Even the whole ones are sticky, as if from spit;
on the air, the scent of just-fermenting fruit
and just-gone deer. Just east, across the lake,
a mile past swamp and dunes, the ocean rolls.
Last year a hurricane flooded the orchard. Months on,
blue crabs walked the less and less brackish lakebed
as the water lilies returned, and the water weed.
The crabs could not last; the orchard grass is back
in soil washed through with salt. A fat green pear
has fallen to the crook of one tree's branches.
I lift it out and balance it on the others,
whole and near-whole, cradled in my shirt.
Cutting them open in the evening kitchen,
we meet the sweetest water, squeezed from between
rough round cells that greet the tongue like grains
of sand, but softer, yielding—exactly the thing
you'd think would come from flowers, in May, across
the lake and swamp, over dunes, through myrtle and pine,
conversing with the ocean—in each pear
a center, fresh and salt, nectar and stone.

Fall Swim

Go on and jump, he says, *it's not that cold.*
He dips both feet in. I sit tight, feel old.
I thought you were the one. He means, the one
who's always up for this, part lake, part human.
I was once. Suddenly I'm not so wild.

He strips down, leaps, is gone, emerges: *Oh,*
it's fine—his voice high-pitched—*no, not that cold.*
Liar. I hug my knees. No way I can
go on and jump—

but then I'm out of pants, shirt, standing chilled
now running—wait—too late to quit the willed
leap from dock to lake. Too cold to recline,
but paddling, moonlit, delirious, shivering—
Oh, right, it's fine—from this night forward, I'll
go on and jump.

Trifoliate Orange

Candy girl, candy girl, give me back my five dollars.
—"Candy Girl," trad.

No apple tree. No blackberries, even,
in the back field. My path well made,
nothing else had drawn me so far,
skirting horse nettles—only these oranges.
Sticky, acidic, some huge, half-dollars,
some smaller, their yellow shadowed with green,
they hung in a thicket of muscular branches,
crowding the woods' edge with crowns of thorns
connected by green in unvarying arcs
like the web between fingers. Who were they made for?
I reached in sideways, dropped into my basket
each pale, flocked sun. Past dusk, I halved them,
sloughed away the slippery seeds,
sliced them in strips and emptied sugar
by cupfuls into the simmering marmalade.
Still it was fierce, more sour than storebought.
Ate it on corncakes alone in the kitchen,
licking my fingers, the places where thorns pricked them
clotted with sugar. Night at the windows.
The ones I missed—sent tumbling from stem,
my reach too short, the branch left shaking—
lay on sparse moss, in fine bamboo grass,
million seeds safe in those soft, bitter skins.

Unhomemaking

Walked through the gap in privet,   stubble of grass cut for hay,
around the curve to where,   before the snow, the yurt rose
like a white mushroom. All week   I'd lain in my new bed, in town,
too sick to stand. I'd imagined   the freezing and melting, freezing
and melting, each time heavier   on the round roof beneath which
I'd slept through the start of winter.   Now the slender lattice
stood, but the rafters had splintered,   canvas ripped—not enough
to hold what had been home   from winter air. Fingers numb,
I finished it, tore away   the ruined roof, circled to fold
the sagging sailcloth wall,   unbolted, unbolted, till all
was gone but the graying platform—   buckled and empty above
the invisible sun of joists—   and on the waterlogged plywood,
a sodden pillow   spilling its downy spores.

Mapping

Every spring she must have seen them returning,
mottled green and marching from deep in the forest
up to the stilts her pale pink house stood on,

even as she kept planting closer to woods' edge,
out from her husband's daylilies, rallying sunlight,
toward the bamboo thicket where medicine bottles

surfaced in earth. Was she surprised as I am
to find the trillium, surfacing too each year?
I follow her paths past bushy azalea and privet,

countless snowdrops, daffodils. And her favorites,
the variegated hostas—for each, she scribbled
a name and a circle to mark the spot she'd planted it,

on typing paper, the flaps of old catalogues, envelopes—
script so quickly written that even her daughters
hardly can read it. Which map is the last one,

the true one? No one can tell. Still I'm walking
as I remember her walking, looking to one side,
the other, ivy invading, pots half-full with rainwater,

then, by the hollow live oak, a single stalk,
leaves the size of my hand, and furled petals
darker than old blood, deeper than new. I lower

my knees to the leaf mold and see, in sepals, the pointing
inner flower she must have seen—she must have
knelt here too, with her trowel, leaned in close

so the cool petals brushed her lips, letting loose
the rare fragrance that lives between her inscrutable
circles—constant, wild, unstoppable red.

Girl at the State Line

I try to fit North and South Carolina next to each other on the fridge, but you'll never catch North snuggling South the way they do on the map. Even if each one's silver border makes it plenty clear they're nothing but neighbors, fences installed around blue plastic backgrounds to keep their business theirs—hemlock or pine, sailboat or ferry, lighthouse or some other lighthouse, sandspur or horseshit—safe in its shining limit.

I hear they've redrawn the boundary, unearthed old markers, updated surveys. Still, maybe these lines are not so sturdy as souvenirs make them; maybe they're real-live silver linings, rickrack trim sewn to the hem of a storebought skirt with the hasty hand of someone whose Saturday evening approaches. Won't last long, those stitches, the way we dance down here—stay all night and don't go home, come dawn step out and look: land that does not brake for state lines, pauses only for rivers, stops only at sea.

Virgil Anderson, border walker, can I pledge allegiance to limit and endlessness both? Heaven's blessings attend you, Virgil, for what is a shuffle but hesitation, sweet indecision? But I've already decided: I've ripped a stitch jumping over that ditch, forsaken hemlock for hemlock, pine for pine, lighthouse for lighthouse, horseshit for what looks, suspiciously, also like horseshit—made my escape in the Wright Brothers' striped, impossible aeroplane, leaving a skywriter's trail to solder the sundered foothills, scattering silver left and right as I pass from piedmont into piedmont into piedmont

I'm going back to North Carolina
And I never expect to see you any more.
—Sheila Kay Adams; trad.

I'm Going Back to North Carolina

Come home with me and kiss me in bright shade
along the bikeway and creek where muscadine
curls over asphalt and sewer line,
covering the surfaces humans have made.
Above us, on the overpass, tar and gravel
car-scattered, but here, blackberries swell
in speckled light, hard green knots of cells
decked in shreds of flower, and still vines travel,

leafing and leaning into sun, as we
lean into their shadow. Three years back we rode
this passage in the dark, an edge in us
crowded with possible fruit, stippled with day.
We cycled through that margin, into a field
of lengthening afternoons, a surety

to last us years together and years apart
from Carolina. Now, held fast in our
habitual sun, we tilt south, needing more—
the shifting light of woods-edge to remind us
of first uncertainty that, tended, turns
into a constant chaos we can start

to make a home in. Let's walk as the wild
grape moves, with curving purpose, out from flared
noon light to shade and back, breathing in
the saving scent of honeysuckle, jewelweed,
summer grasses and our sun-warmed hair,
dizzying our senses, pulling us toward
each other's verdant bodies, summoning
a salve, a word to keep us: we live here.

Unfinished Story

Before her brother lost his shoe in the pluff mud,
before they went crabbing with rotten chicken necks,
before her sister fell in the creek at the ditch-bank,
there was this: once, on the bus from school, my mother
read past her stop, till the end of the route. Slouched down,
her knees against the seat, a tunnel of story
enfolded her; she didn't notice her house
go past, or else it wasn't there. Then no one was left
but her and the nearly golden light
of late afternoon, glancing off brown leather seats,
dust motes she did not see. Work done, the driver
parked the bus and checked back through the rows,
receptionist thumbing past emptied files,
searching for the errant slip of paper, the last to-do
of the day. *Little girl!* He called her back
to the evening, traced the finished route
down quiet streets. She watched from the clouded
window, crying. The book lay closed on her legs,
its name obscured by her crossed hands
so even when I ask her what it was called,
I cannot see the title: now the only story's
the ride home, made backward, infused with fear.
Her parents, where are they? They might be angry.
She is alone, the world's changed, nothing
has come true, and this is where
the story ends: before she reaches home.

Limax maximus

for Richard S. Fox

I learned to fix a specimen with pins
in hardened wax inside a sardine can
and slice the length of speckled gray-brown skin,
its slime diffused by beer. Lab alcohol
would leave them rigid, said the biologist,
who'd promised this would be one science project
the other home-schooled kids, the prudish moms
would not forget—and so we drowned the slugs
in Miller Lite. I pulled the mantle back
and made a slit, used tweezers to extract
the tiny shell, a pinky fingernail,
reminder of their closest, shellbound kin.

Next I pinned aside the body wall,
revealing pebble shapes—peach, violet, sand,
the oblong organs nestled in their places.
Who knew they'd be so colorful inside?
I labeled aorta, lung, albumen gland,
hermaphroditic duct meandering
the body's length, combining male and female.
With a lot of luck, he said, as we watched one slug
rippling its single foot across the glass
of its aquarium, I'd come across
a pair of them, dangling deep in nighttime woods.
He'd seen them once. I wanted this so badly

I saw it too: as they had found each other,
I would find their gleaming form, draw close
as imperceptibly they recreated
each other, either from either. When two of them

decided, he had said, they set out on
a stately trek together up a tree trunk,
their pedal glands secreting slime to smooth
the path, then found a safe, high span of branch.
They circled each other, making a silver crown
of mucus over bark, moved close to lick
each other's mantles with their radulae
and oral tentacles, laid ring on ring,

over minutes, over even hours,
till the mass was strong, and they began to exude
a double-stranded rope of sticky mucus,
thick enough to hold the weight of two.
They dropped—descended into empty air,
bobbing as the pliant rope held firm,
and each extended from the gonopore
(a tiny hole at the side of the head—I'd seen it,
had penciled in its name in careful script)—
a flared, white penis unlike anything
I thought of when I thought of penises.
It twined around the other's, making a sphere

itself flanked by the fluted penis combs:
a space for each to take the other's sperm.
When they were done, they climbed up through the air,
ingesting the rope as they ascended it—
for once, leaving no trail. They reached the branch,
cleaving the crown they'd made, as within each one,
sperm moved from retracted penis toward the eggs,
which traveled down to meet it as the slugs
slid over limb, trunk, ground, their ways diverging
as they sought a place—the V between two roots,
between a rock and soil—to lay a mass
of pearly eggs to hatch, in time, as slugs.

Grooved feet gliding over the earth, they left
a trail of slime and kin—impermanent trace

of where they'd been and how they came to be,
whose human complement no one explained
with such a lack of fear or innuendo,
such wonderment. Transported, I saw them live—
adorned with ruffled combs and white penes,
suspended in moonlight—glistening, mottled bodies,
slow aerialists on their gloss trapeze.

Knot

Like arms of an anemone, the way
they wave in water, but more tightly packed:
I hunched above my knee and pushed aside
the fleshy, threadlike tendrils of the wart,
the fiber minions of a multitude
I couldn't conquer. I'd tried scraping at them
a little, just to see, and found they bled
for ages while I pressed against the spot
with a piece of toilet paper—which I must,
I thought, or else they'd spread. How had it come,
this singularity containing many?
I didn't know, but it was of me—was me.

Then, on the blacktop, by the three big oaks
where we ran laps in gym, I took it out:
realized I was headed for the ground
and pushed into a slide. The wart sheared off
on asphalt, left my knee to bleed and bleed
and then to heal, no scar. It didn't return.
A triumph I could hardly brag about,
but I'd ended it, that little wayward knot—
had rallied chance and the will to steer in hard
earthward, meet the ground with all my weight
and let it round me down to one, to naught.

The Waxweed Girl

He brought me a rose; its velvet petals bled.
I wore that rose behind my ear all day
though it weighted me, off-kilter, too big for my head,
the rose he brought. Its velvet petals bled
on the hallway floor. I left a trail of red
that no one followed but him: I was his prey.
He tracked the scent of velvet petals' blood
I wore, that rose behind my ear all day.

Wand

We opened the wrappers of yellow lightsticks
and broke the plastic tubes—the sound
like knuckles popping, satisfying—to let
the glow loose. Threw them high
into the dark, to see their fluorescence against
the clouded sky. No moon. Hers had just fallen
to the lawn again when I tossed mine up
and it didn't come down. Sideways, twenty feet high,
it moved along the air toward the branches
of the pecan trees, drew a neon trail
over the monkey bars my dad had built, then
dropped. She ran for the house, scared.
But I was busy: how had mine traveled? A bat
must have carried it off—flown thirty feet to be convinced
this was no snack—and let it fall. Triumphant,
already retelling the story to myself, I followed her
in to dessert, to the lit, warm space of my family,
suddenly terribly dull, even as the wand, touched
by the night world, began to fade in my hand.

Proem

Before our friends showed up for pre-prom wine—
or was it grape juice—and dainty snacks, we posed
in his parents' yard, in misting rain. From the porch,
his mother eyed us through the lens of his
expensive camera: in black and white,
we're standing close beneath the somber curve
of the umbrella, earnest, thankful the shot's
not straight-on. I'm quizzical; he tilts
his head toward me, puzzled—it's a stance
we both find useful. But while we squint, our bodies
stay our bodies: earthly, matter-of-fact,
they tell the camera to go ahead,
record us. We look up to his mother's gaze,
and from that lucky angle, find ourselves
almost convinced that this is what we are.

Strapless

Fearing my nipples would betray themselves
beneath their bodice, I donned a strapless bra.
But it revolted: slipping from my breasts,
dismounted them, inched down my waist to where
it rested, chaste, symmetric, satisfied.
"See the miraculous brassiere! It cuts
her clean in half: and yet she lives!" I died
all night, again and again, as it marked the span
of my torso, cleaving hours into minutes—
ten, five, two—till I excused myself
and left, face stricken (what must he have thought?).
I never had the thought to take it off.
Instead, in the bathroom mirror's sudden glare,
I wrestled it again up over my breasts,
then darted back to the gym, to mirror-ball
shimmer and slow dance, praying to be taken
for a girl, whether or not I knew I was.

Dishwashing

Dregs of red wine are left in my grandmother Swannie's
crystal glasses that surely were made for some finer
vintage, tiny flowers circling their lips,
stained and serene next to coffee cups, stacked plates.
Now I run warm water into one glass and
poke at the stubborn wine in its curving bowl.
Pushing the loosening edges of crimson feels like
putting my finger in somebody's belly button,

an innie, looking for lint, a lode of it, barely
visible, dark in the dark, satisfaction of scraping
something from something. But *belly button*'s too close to
sin, she'd have said, too private, almost cussing,
all those covered-up parts had better stay covered
outside the narrow occasions when being naked's
sanctioned. If the glass has a navel, though, it
can't be somebody else's: squirming, they'd say she was

right, my grandmother, that's what makes someone's privates
private. Even a dishwasher's clinical touch,
up to the elbows in soapsuds, would set them off, and
since it's been proved you cannot tickle your ownself,
this must be mine: I must have been wearing red,
lots of it, velvety, wine-dark red that rolls itself
into the body's crevices, makes itself comfy—
or else I am reopening, not aberrance

but reminder: this is the bowl you collect in,
portal to inside, archaic, these are the vital
dregs that turn you into yourself. You know
all of the curses. Speaking their names, gather your
sins, incremental as lint, and as small, and consider:

are they yours, or have you just been keeping them?
Either way, you're self-cleaning: time and your two hands,
elbow grease, god bless, and a little warm water.

Shade

Pushing the garbage bin out to the street
I squeezed past the cedar and saw in my path
my legs and skirt cast on the packed dirt, transparent
among the tree's blanketed shadow and light.
Near-opaque echoes of evergreen leaves
stippled my fainter shape, feathered me through.
I'd seen how this happens—how tree trunk and bough
and the tiniest plants lap and blend at the ground,
their bodies made lighter or larger, revealed—
but never my own shadow lighter than trees',
refracted and shifting, no less or more
than all whose shades lie over soft forest floor.

Crosses

I.

It's true I'd been seduced: in high-school biology
we read of Mendel crossing pea plants

for a glimpse of their methods, the flowers' colors shifting
in gradually discernible patterns. Who could remain impassive,

objective? For dissection, everyone chose their own animal
from the catalogue—a mink, a squid—like ordering prizes

from the fundraiser book but these had once been alive, the mammals
pre-skinned to disguise that fact. I appealed; while they poked with razors,

I diagrammed corn stalks, cross-sections projected
onto the dirty classroom floor from slides, color-coded cells

so spacious inside it seemed they were offering up
all of their secrets.

II.

That year a new cat, mottled calico, showed up in our yard
and was coaxed to eat, me watching from ten feet away, then five,

before she made the barn loft hers and allowed me to feed her
from the hole where the ladder came up. If I stood

on a middle rung with only head and shoulders
showing, she'd let me stroke her back, even purr,

her half-tail waving its radius.
No chance she'd be spayed. When she had kittens, I recited

the crosses, reverent, as if I could speak them
to Mendel himself: one with a whole tail, one with half,

another with half, and one with none. The kittens were skittish
and wilder than she was, climbing the skinny persimmon

back of the barn to escape me. Two we gave
to neighbors, one was snatched by a hawk; the one left

had a half-long tail. The triumph of that.

III.

Midsummer, I could not guess which
of the tiny heirloom zinnias would be red,

orange, magenta, and which the paler colors
I like less. The seeds pushed the potting soil aside

with their paired leaves, their hundreds, and he,
faithfully following instructions, planted every one

in the small space, close, too close. Now with the sungolds
and the leggy, half-grown zinnias, we disagree: him unwilling

to call a hybrid any less intrusive than the new shifting
of genes from creature to creature; my counterpoint—

the seasons of tries made over by hand,
the number of feet each family requires

to avoid cross-pollination, the hoped-for surprise—
not enough to move him, but which

is more important, stopping, or proving myself
stubborn as he is? It's all in knowing when to stop

meddling, my love, my logical. Romanced
by the changes (one with no tail, two with half a tail,

one with a whole, boring tail) we forget our own: having shaped
these plants, we must tend them as we tend

each other, give water, give room,
climb the steps to the house and open the door,

leave the garden to win the argument.

Bonaparte Crossing the Rhine

When he had gone I sat and played alone,
remembering how I'd told him "Go to hell"
and feeling dismal. Who knew I'd recall
that melody? It marched in slow and fine
and brought back not his body but the sound
of notes we'd played, an echo, rise, and swell
that swept on up the fretboard as I fell
in love—with him? I must've lost my mind.
I thought I'd take the player, would as soon
sin as settle for less. But memory serves
me well, suggests another, better plan:
it holds the music—never mind the man—
and I've been playing long enough to prove
that this arrangement's fine. I'll keep the tune.

Strike

My father cusses under his breath but loud.
He's cut himself. *Are you okay?* I say—
I can't get close enough to see how bad.
I know he will
not answer, and I step back. Still,

from the okra, *Maybe you should stop,* I say.
Maybe I will. He hauls off, whacks the fence
with the clippers—splinters shatter, red from gray—
and walks back toward the bean rows, hands full of wires.
Holding nothing, I head to the house.

He finds me close to supper time. *Sorry
I ran you off. Short fuse.*
There's something he wants me
to see; I want
to say okay. He opens the desk, pulls out

the severed head of a rattlesnake, mounted
on a pin. He got it out West. It's meant
for the lapel of someone clueless, mean—
but he bought it instead. He holds the head
in his bandaged hand,

says, *I wanted people to see how fragile they are.*
I lean away: it smells like a dead thing, the snake,
the fangs like sewing sharps, gently bowed, bare,
waiting to strike, stock-still
as we are. We stare as if it will.

Girl at the State Line

Better than getting both pound cake and pie for dessert, the way she told it: her father stopped the Ford up at the Carolina line, on 25, granite rockface to either side marking the channel they'd blasted for the highway. She stepped from the truck. "I stood with one foot in each state, and my daddy took my picture!" The photograph's long gone, but I picture her there, midday, mid-drive, by the sign proclaiming

WELCOME TO NORTH CAROLINA
NORTH CAROLINA STATE LINE.

Left foot in South, right foot in North, between her patent shoes she finds the border, ghost-line superimposed on scrubby grass, turned invisible where her shadow falls. In her yellow dress, she looks up as he records her crossing: she's smiling the way she did before I knew her, she's a miracle, above her the mountain is chiseled with hints of her Jesus's face, and below, made giant, erasing the line, she stands— the girl who spans two states.

Green Man

He will not subside,   won't slip into leaf-mold;

he lived in the woods   where my father found him:

a weathered plank   with waiting sockets.

He carried him home   and carved the cedar:

a narrow nose   nestled in red crest

lichen, lips   like his own, and scuppernong

beard; bronze ivy   to crown his brows.

Last, he split walnuts   and wedged each half

into its hollow,   hallowed his face

with cool creek water,   and called him whole.

Then, as he'd promised,   he posted him north.

Dry moss crackled   in the bubble mailer;

wide eyes emerged   to watch me while

I made him a place   in my winter house

and bade him rest.   Now, as I breathe,

a verdant current   fills craven air:

he exhales, his mouth   speaks moss, makes leaf.

And Not Look Back

Hand me down my walking cane
I'm gonna leave on the midnight train
                              —James Bland

Pull the front door shut and drop the latch.
Hand me down my walking cane. I won't look back.

You catch a glimpse or two; he steals them away—
keep hold of what you can, and don't look back.

I've done it all my life—kept misery
at bay with one firm line: Don't look back.

If anybody asks you where I've gone
say I've left on the midnight train and won't look back.

Rosin up the bow for one more tune.
How can I play this refrain and not look back?

Look neither back nor forward—that's the way
to love. Drink up your wine, and don't look back.

Is that you, standing just beyond the porch light?
Well, step in out of the rain, and don't look back.

Stitch

Making myself content with what was half
plenty, good but never what you'd call
fine tailoring, I worried out a hole
in what I knew of love—don't move too much
in this, your only shirt, it'll all unstitch—
and the gap sewed itself into myself.
What's missing now's the feel of missing something.
Should I be wary, lacking it, or find
this double absence sweet? We've cut and pinned
our pieces, we have ripped out hems, unseaming—
but in our rending, not a knot is sundered
that we cannot baste down, sew up, make right.
I pinch all I've held apart—in case of what?—shut.
Now press. Now stitch. Now billow: splendid.

I'll eat when I'm hungry,
I'll drink when I'm dry,
Get to feeling much better, gonna sprout wings and fly.
                                    —*Tommy Jarrell*

To Do in the New Year

Be ribbon. Be bone.
Be lace. Be stone.
Make a bow of yourself—no,
make of yourself a bear.
Furl fur, steer windward.
Make of yourself
a byre. Shimmer. Ray,
then bow: ends
unravel, ravel,
unfurl. Make of yourself
a curl, a funnel. Bay.
Whine. Say
soon, daffodils
will, miracle
gone before we know.
And that is how time.
And that is how.
Be still. Steal in. Stare.
Make of yourself
a string unwinding
forever, fire,
make of yourself
a constellation of obstacles, make

inroads, make a solution
of sunshine, be seed.
Cede. Be siloed.
Cease for a while, be
quilted; in creases,
fall seaward. From hulls,
rise, riled up, increase, raise up
sounds of your name
in water, make yourself
golden, yield.

The Royal Typewriter Company Delivers by Parachute, 1927

So what if it was all publicity—
the genius plan of one man, George Ed Smith,
designed to sell the typewriter to us,
the secretaries of America?
I tell you, when that Royal floated down,
at first a speck emerging from the plane—
a parachute, and hung from that, a crate
that hid the black machine—I felt myself
go light, imagining the sleek design
of these new portables, their round black keys
and what they'd do if they could withstand gravity,
buoyed along, if they could clatter out
the sentences that they loved best: each word
imprinted from their silken, inky ribbons
onto the sky, then spilling from the crates
and floating earthward, even to towns that Smith
had not deemed fit for blessing. Everyone
stepped back as that first Royal neared the earth,
and I wished I could stop, and never see
it land. It did. They pulled away the slats
to show its shining finish, glowing keys,
and everybody's boss could hardly stop
his girl from her insistence that she must
have one of those. Of course I got one too.
But all the stock reports it has produced,
the stiff condolences, official deeds,
are nothing when I think of all the words
I almost saw, the ordinary air
filling with silk and possibility.

Sunday

The blue and white dress
is perfect to wear on Sunday, mowing the lawn.
The blue and white dress—
its stripes skim over skin and only suggest
hips, thighs, sweet shaking obvious
to the mower-pusher and the mower-pusher alone
in the blue and white dress.

Nesting

First time she went to hang her clothes
in the windy yard, on the line,
she startled a nest of whirring wasps
between the back door and the screen.

Hundreds of sharp round abdomens,
an undulance of shine and wing,
had built their mud and paper home,
hung from the screen-door spring.

She shut the door quick, and watched them fly
from a tear in the screen, toward the sun,
but next day they were back. She took up her broom
to whack the thing from its anchor-line.

The anchor snapped with the first two strikes
and with the third, the nest fell,
carried down on a waspbuzz wake.
It rested on the sill.

Now they'd go, she thought, and closed
the door on the wreck she'd made.
But they swarmed the spring where their home had hung,
waiting in the shade.

She doused them with water, vinegar, soap,
hoping they'd burn and take off,
but they hardly noticed: just buzzed, settled down,
their silence a waspy *fuck off.*

She learned to walk under the ghost of the nest,
careful, her head held low.
No stings rained down, so she went in and out,

her arms full of newly washed clothes.

As fall came on, if she left the door
open, they'd crawl right in.
Where could they go in the snowy cold?
She couldn't keep back the wind.

She caught one with a cup and paper,
one day in the dining room,
and carried it out the laundry door
to let it fly from the rim.

She lifted the page; the wasp perched on the edge—
antennae waved in the sun—
and looked around, but didn't fly.
It crawled toward her thumb.

She threw the cup and paper down
on shadow-splashed concrete:
porcelain cracked, and fragments scratched
over stone, just missing her feet.

She raised her eyes in time—the wasp
was lifting from her sight.
It led the rest. In a whirring line,
they flew from her, toward the light.

When the Fire Comes Down
from Heaven

I hold a finger up to fix the span
of every bird whose shadow crosses mine,
seeking one who echoes the divine
proportion. None fits perfectly, none can.
But one soars close. Its shining sears my forehead,
that gold encompassing all opposites—
pasture, stream, the house where my love tats lace—
two equal filaments of cotton thread

held on two silver shuttles, a shawl she'll wear
when I tread home across the darkening meadow,
ablaze with the mark the hawk has made on me.
As I trace it on her skin, we'll know each other
as well as our hinged and mortal symmetry
allows, shadow to body, body to shadow.

Honeysuckle

For scant weeks in spring when the ground has had time to
    get warmer,
and all the white flowers whose forms are so hard to imagine

are coming to bloom, and the air smells each day of some newness,
a sweetness whose name, like the scent, flags the tip of the tongue

then leaves, leads me onward, leads bees on, leads moths, leads
    small flies
(for who knows which beast every flower is meant to attract

and who can collect each one's name?), I breathe in as much of
the air as will flow through my lungs before—sudden, persistent—

you lower down over the piedmont, imparting a one-noted
sweetness that has to content us all summer, for only

a rare other fragrance can cut through those curtains of sugar.

Early Blackberries

Years since I first mistook the elder trees for
poison ivy, my little brother laughs as
I shrink back again from the jagged leaves.
Crossing the creekbed

near the old bridge—rusting nails, and the bright ones
I thought were dragonflies when I was younger,
black wings, blue-green bodies shining like thread.
Edge of the neighbor's

land, we step from woods into brambles thick with
leaves we lift aside for the few ripe berries.
Soon I can't see him, but his singing travels—
Blackberry picking,

blackberry picking—voice so new to breaking
over the thicket's thorns and shed white flowers,
fruit no one else eats save the birds. He must set
out by his lonesome

every day as the sun sinks lower, humming,
wading through canes that score his legs with scarlet—
what does he think about as evening comes on?
"Make way for the guide!"

Heading up toward supper, him in the lead:
dimming woods, the creek keeps up its eddying,
dark snaky water opaque now, damselflies
gone in the twilight.

He holds out an arm for me as I cross, then,
one big hand on his bowl of berries, jumps from
high bank to low, lands solid, and no, he
doesn't spill any.

Roustabout

Oh, it's where'd you get your brand-new shoes,
and the dress that you wear so fine?

Say truly, God, are you the kind
to wear a sequin? To unwind
a length of lace and baste it round
the hem of every handsome gown?
Must you send such silver down
the sweep of every dress you own?

Or will you walk in coarser thread—
a hand of salt, a hand of dirt
to scatter wide as on you tread,
wiping dust on a homespun shirt?
Do you hop high by moonlit pears?
Do you wreak mischief with the deer?

Let buttons shine from stubbled field,
let mud wash out, let flax dry fast.
Let pears be burnished, lace outlast
both salt and starch. Let all be held
aloft, alight, in your slight grasp,
a skein, a spool, a well-spun spell.

Overture

If all of the stars had a million guitars,
And the moon were the girl that I loved...
        —"Waltzing on Top of the World,"
              Jim Reeves

If all of the stars had a million guitars,
their notes sifting down through the poplars and firs,
and you offered, I'd say, "Sure, the next waltz is yours,"
but I know my science: the stars are just stars.

If all of my wishes turned out to be kisses—
and just between us, I'd have bushels and bales,
to last all our evenings clear through to Sunday—
but time counting wishes is time counting losses.

For all of the stars could lay down their guitars
and, just like that, grant no more earthly requests,
no flowers and fine shoes, no scent of the rain,
no buttery biscuits, no bed by the fire—
so I'll lay down my science and count up my senses.
Come lie down beside me, and I won't complain.

June Swim

If I had a needle and thread, as fine as I could sew,
I'd sew my true love to my side, and down this creek I'd go.
                              —"Jubilee," Jean Ritchie

Where one stream curves between the middle islands,
foot-deep and fast, clear muscle moving eastward,

he anchored us and held me as I floated—
as little fishes nipped, as he cried *Oh*

at each, then played at stoicism—*What fish?*
Then I put my feet down on the riverbed,

laced my arms through his so he could feel
the water pull his body to its length,

passing him on all sides, while he lay still
and wavered by the moving stream. Who else

had thought to hold me here as I reclined,
or tug me one way by an arm, and back

by a leg, so I could feel the water peal
along me like cool bells, that giant kiss

I used to feel midwater, self-propelled?
But this one knows: it's him and river. The Haw

insists its seaward course, insists we float,
be flown. We won't say no. I take his hand

and we lift our feet to let the current go.

Sprout Wings and Fly

Like a watermelon seed,
the geologist said,
if you can find one of those these days,
and hold it between your fingers, squeeze:
like this, the continental plates
are squeezing one plate out from between
two others. I am no plate, but
I feel the weight of continents,
resist, as schist, but then
give in, be squeezed, and feel
the slip: pressed, launched from myself,
heaven in a coconut shell
or hell in a handbasket
but finally, catapulted
from what may be my own fingers—
If I am my own torment—
If I am God, the capital-H hand
that presses not to crush
but to propel, palms like dinner plates,
palms like granite; the capital-G glad
mouth that knows better than to eat
lest a seed grow in the belly,
replication when the prayer
was for shift; that anyhow needs
no such nourishment, that instead purses, spits
self from self, if only for a brief respite,
for the list will never be short enough
that I could stand and walk free of it—
If I am standing next to my faults,
starting from solid ground—
if I get to feeling much better
in spite of myself,

in a spate of say yes—yes to you,
little satchel of sums, little seed sprouted,
gone winged, some bright morning, I'm gonna,
any day, today, now—

Hush

Cries of katydids make a pool of sound,
    filling up the invisible bowl of night, whose
sill you rest on, spelled by stars' faint light.
    Now the pestle moon will grind your troubles
down to thinnest powder against the grooves of
    those coarse cries, and now a chirring wind sends
trials to pasture, scatters them past the fence.
    You remain. Slide down that singing surface,
spilling into it, like the black-eared kitten,
    who, once she has eaten, steps into the blue
porcelain bowl, curls up, and never thinking
    she herself could be eaten, sleeps and sleeps.

Some Songs and Tunes

Most of the songs and tunes this book draws on have been played by many different people. These are some of the songs, and some of the versions, I have had in mind.

"Green Ford Blues." Virgil Anderson.... *On the Tennessee Line: Old Time Banjo from the Upper Cumberland.* County LP 777, 1980.

"Make Me a Pallet on Your Floor." Mississippi John Hurt. *Recorded Live in Concert.* Castle Pulse, PLSCD 681, 2004.

"Candy Girl." Uncle Bunt Stephens. *Nashville: The Early String Bands, Vol. 1.* County Records CD 3521, 2000.

"The Carolina Lady." Dillard Chandler. *High Atmosphere.* Rounder Records 0028, LP, 1974.

"I'm Going Back to North Carolina." Sheila Kay Adams. Live performance, North Carolina Museum of Art, July 2004.

"Old East Virginia." Morgan Sexton. *Shady Grove.* June Appal JA 066C, 1992.

"My Home's Across the Blue Ridge Mountains." The Carolina Tar Heels. *The Carolina Tar Heels.* Old Homestead OHCS 113, LP, 1978. Originally released in 1929.

"The Waxweed Girl." David and Lucy Pricket. Max Hunter Folk Song Collection, Missouri State, cat. #0008 (MFH #670).

"The Story of the Knoxville Girl." The Blue Sky Boys. *Original and Great: Early Authentic Country Recordings.* Camden CAL 797, LP, 1964. Recorded in 1937.

"Bonaparte Crossing the Rhine." Fuzzy Mountain String Band. *Summer Oaks & Porch.* Rounder Records 0035, LP, 1973.

"Hand Me Down My Walking Cane."

James Bland (composer), 1880.

Ernest V. Stoneman, Edison Records 5297, 1927.

"Marching Jaybird." Etta Baker and Cora Phillips. *Carolina Breakdown.* Music Maker 56, CD, 2005.

"Heaven's Aeroplane." Hobart Smith. *In Sacred Trust: The 1963 Fleming Brown Tapes.* Smithsonian Folkways SFW40141, 2005.

"Uncloudy Day." Hobart Smith. *In Sacred Trust: The 1963 Fleming Brown Tapes.* Smithsonian Folkways SFW40141, 2005.

"Shake Sugaree." Elizabeth Cotten. *Shake Sugaree.* Smithsonian Folkways SFW40147, 2004.

"Police." Tommy Jarrell, Fred Cockerham, & Oscar Jenkins. *Down to the Cider Mill.* County Records LP 713, 1968.

"Tribulations." E. C. & Orna Ball. *E. C. Ball with Orna Ball & the Friendly Gospel Singers.* Rounder CD 6311577, 1996.

"The Curtains of Night." The Tenneva Ramblers. *The Tenneva Ramblers.* Puritan 3001, LP, 1972. Recorded in 1928.

"Roustabout."

Fred Cockerham. *Clawhammer Banjo, Vol. 2.* County Records CD 2717, 2003. Originally released in 1969.

Dink Roberts. *Dink Roberts.* Field Recorders Collective FRC 209, 2009. Recorded in 1978.

Josh Thomas. Recorded in 1970.

"Waltzing on Top of the World." Jim Reeves. *Have I Told You Lately That I Love You?* RCA Camden LP CAS842(e), 1969.

"Jubilee." Jean Ritchie. *Jean Ritchie Singing the Traditional Songs of Her Kentucky Mountain Family.* Elektra EKLP-2, 1952.

"Cindy Gal." Joe Thompson. *Family Tradition.* Rounder 2161, CD, 1999.

"Drunken Hiccups" (also "Jack of Diamonds"). Tommy Jarrell. *Tommy Jarrell, Vol. 1,* with Paul Brown and Mike Seeger. Field Recorders Collective FRC 211, 2009.

"I'll Fly Away." Albert E. Brumley (composer), 1929.

"All the Pretty Little Horses." Pete Seeger. *Golden Slumbers: Lullabies from Far and Near.* Book-Records Soundbook 1020, LP, 1972.

"Whole Heap A Little Horses." Texas Gladden. *Southern Journey Volume 2: Ballads and Breakdowns—Songs From The Southern Mountains.* Alan Lomax Collection. Rounder Records CD 1702, 1997.

"Say, Darling, Say." Tommy Jarrell. *Rainbow Sign.* County Records CO-2725-CD, 1999. Originally released in 1986.

* The epigraph for "Piedmont" is from John McPhee's *In Suspect Terrain*, Farrar, Straus and Giroux, 1991, p. 128 (first published in 1983).

CPSIA information can be obtained
at www.ICGtesting.com
Printed in the USA
BVHW08s0515220818
525120BV00001B/29/P